TAW VALL

FROM DREAM TO STEAM

Ian McDonald

Midland Publishing
Limited

Copyright 1993 Ian E. McDonald

Published by
Midland Publishing Limited
24 The Hollow, Earl Shilton
Leicester, LE9 7NA, England

ISBN 1-85780-011-7

Printed in England by
Printhaus Graphique Limited
Round Spinney, Northampton

Designed by
Midland Publishing Limited

Front cover photograph:
Taw Valley at Chart Leacon, Ashford,
on Friday 13th September 1991.

Title page photograph:
34027 on the North West Coast Express,
Anglesey, 1990. Steve Kirk

Back Cover photograph:
Taw Valley at Folkestone Harbour in
September 1991.

CONTENTS

ACKNOWLEDGEMENTS

As an active member of the loco's support crew, I thought I knew quite a bit about No 34027 *Taw Valley*. However, in the course of researching the portrayal of the career of *Taw Valley* since its recovery from South Wales, I have become aware of how much more there was to the story than I had previously been aware of.

The tale of how the locomotive came to be chosen has an element of romance that would not disgrace a Mills & Boon novel and without the contributions, both large and small, of a great number of people, this story would never have happened. It involves the people who started the locomotive on the long road back to an operational state, those who have nursed and looked after her since those early days, and the professionals who have offered assistance and guidance both throughout the long process of the engine's restoration and subsequently as the locomotive has performed on BR tracks and preserved lines around Britain.

There are also drivers, firemen, fitters, inspectors and many ordinary enthusiasts whose daily life revolved, and for some still revolves, around this particular steam locomotive. Many have assisted in all the unseen activities required to run a locomotive on the main line and others have travelled from all over the country to support the railtours or to see the locomotive on whatever line she is running. To all of these and to those who helped in the production of this book I can say no more than, thank you.

Special thanks go to Liz Hitchen, Bert Hitchen, Brian Cooke, Roger Scanlon, the 34027 *Taw Valley* Support Crew, Steve G.McColl, Brian Morrison, Chris Milner and all at Midland Publishing.

Finally, thanks go to the one person without whose support and encouragement I couldn't have done any of this – my wife – Angie.

Ian McDonald   June 1993

FOREWORD

Bulleid meant nothing to me until 1966 when my grandfather, an engine driver, took me to London Waterloo. After an hour or so of looking at familiar and unfamiliar engines he talked us on to a 'Merch' as far as Basingstoke, joining the crew later on a 'Light' back to Waterloo. I think it was 'Clovelly' dirty and forlorn. I, and I think my grandfather, had never travelled so fast on a steam engine before. It was 25 years before I would experience a Bulleid again.

Once I had shaken off years of indoctrination that God only looked after the LMS, I grew to appreciate Bulleid's work and the subsequent development of it. Having read one book about him I have always unashamedly copied him in one respect; I always have a crucifix on my wall and having thought about it, I think he must have had an inspired guardian angel at least.

I first saw *Taw Valley* in Barry scrapyard, ironically only months before Liz and Bert Hitchen went there. It was in a sad state and just one of a number of similar hulks. I little thought that it, or for that matter any, of the engines there would one day be the flagship for the return of steam to the Southern.

Taw Valley is a marketing man's nightmare and a motive power man's delight. As Ian McDonald relates, it was never famous but it has always (apart from one incident) been reliable. When I served on a small aircraft carrier we were always being asked, 'Is it like Ark Royal, is it famous?'. Our answers, the printable ones anyway, usually centred on, 'Sort of, we're just too busy to get on television'. Similar things must have been said of *Taw Valley*, but they've certainly heard of her now. *Taw Valley* has deservedly built up a large following who come back again and again to be entertained.

I have taken part in many of the West Country wanderings with *Taw Valley*, some of which will only be related in the distant future to protect the guilty! I've enjoyed many miles on her footplate but most of all I've enjoyed the company of her support crew, particularly the stalwarts; Bert, Liz, Brian, Roger, Neil, Steve, John and of course Ian. We've all shared a few harsh words, lots of laughs, a few misty eyed moments and most of all, the realisation of some of our earliest ambitions, thanks to a remarkable 'unfamous' locomotive.

I commend this book as being not only an excellent chronicle of the exploits of *Taw Valley*, but because of the contributions of the author to the engine's success. Not only is Ian a railwayman and exceptional photographer, he is guaranteed to be doing the filthiest job about the loco!

Steve McColl
InterCity Special Projects

***Taw Valley* leaves Shrewsbury for Crewe. The MN tender can be seen to good effect and the detail differences between it and *Taw Valley's* own tender can be clearly seen. Saturday 20th May 1989**

INTRODUCTION

Much has been written about and many words have been used in animated discussion on the topic of the 'Bulleid Pacifics'. They were the 'best thing since sliced bread'; they were a 'fitters nightmare'; they would 'pull and run like the wind'; you didn't know whether you were in forward or backward gear at any given time; they caught fire with monotonous regularity; the list is endless. Then the decision came to rebuild both classes on more conventional lines. Gone were the innovative design features and in their place was a locomotive of extremely handsome lines, slightly heavier, just as powerful and if not able to run like the wind then certainly like a very strong breeze. The fitters had an easier time but the drivers had slightly more to do in preparation whilst the firemen still had a boiler that would produce as much steam as required and when required but could also eat the coal if not driven or fired correctly. All the 'Merchant Navy' class locomotives were eventually rebuilt but not all of the lighter 'West Country'/'Battle of Britain' Pacifics. Both types lasted until the end of steam on the Southern.

34027 *Taw Valley*, a 'West Country' class Pacific, was rebuilt in 1957 – the second of the class to be outshopped in this condition. It was, however, never famous. It wasn't the last of its class in service; it never did 100mph down Wellington Bank; it never went on a trip to the USA, nor did it tour the antipodes. It wasn't the last steam locomotive in active service even on its own region; it wasn't a good engine but likewise it wasn't a bad engine. It had only one stroke of good fortune in its brief life; when it was withdrawn it was sold to the Woodham Brothers, Scrap Merchants of Barry Island, South Wales. There it lay with a motley collection of other relics from the steam era for some 15 years; slowly rotting in the salt laden sea air, unloved, uncared for and surplus to requirements.

This is where the story really starts. In 1979 Liz and Bert Hitchen with their old Alsatian dog Hamish, were on a touring holiday of Wales. Being in the area, Bert, a

former fitter at the old Lancashire & Yorkshire Railway's Mirfield Shed and regular volunteer on the North Yorkshire Moors Railway, brought Liz down to Barry to visit that graveyard of steam and to take a few photographs of the remaining locomotives. Liz recalls that the day was not especially nice and had been somewhat cold and wet. It was that sort of day that darkens the spirit and seemed to make the silent denizens of the docks brood all the more under the constant drizzle from the leaden grey South Wales sky. Towards late afternoon a faint trace of sunshine broke from under the lowering clouds but the sombre mood of the place had already got to Liz as she followed Bert up and down the serried ranks of locomotives withdrawn, neglected and awaiting their fate. Not that Bert had noticed, he was busy climbing over the rotting carcases and photographing the rows of silent engines. Liz called up to Bert to hurry him along so they could go, as she didn't like the place at all and added that if only she could, it was her dream to take one of these abandoned hulks and breath life back into it.

The rest as they say, is history. The 'abandoned hulk' Bert was standing on was 34027 *Taw Valley*. The locomotive was duly inspected, pronounced fit for restoration and was bought by Bert for Liz as her birthday present in January 1980.

At that time there were no tenders for a Bulleid Pacific in the yard so a tender off a BR Standard was purchased with a view to rebuilding it. Eventually this tender, now on the NYMR was rebuilt and is to be used behind BR Standard Class 4 4-6-0 75014, itself presently undergoing restoration at Grosmont.

Taw Valley was taken to the North Yorkshire Moors Railway where restoration commenced. It continued at the East Lancashire Railway and was finally completed on the Severn Valley Railway. On 11th September 1987 steam was raised for the first time since 1964. She hauled her first train on 26th September. After a full repaint over the winter and spring, 34027 emerged on 4th June 1988 to be officially renamed by Liz at a ceremony

in Kidderminster Station on the Severn Valley Railway.

In November 1988, the decision was made to bring 34027 up to main line standard. After more hard work, including borrowing a tender whilst her own was finished, repainting and re-running-in, the locomotive ventured onto British Rail for the first time in 25 years on 15th May 1989 when her main line certificate was obtained. Since then the locomotive has frequently run on British Rail lines.

This book chronicles the life and times of *Taw Valley* in words and pictures. We begin with some glimpses of the engine's career with both the Southern Railway and BR, in both its original and rebuilt condition. We then trace the loco's subsequent rise from a forlorn hulk in Barry scrapyard, through the various stages of restoration to the rebirth of *Taw Valley* as one of the stars of the preservation movement, giving pleasure to thousands on its travels and appearances on both the main line and preserved railways.

All photographs featured in this book were taken by the author unless otherwise stated. Where the author was on BR property to take photographs for this book, he was there with BR's consent.

FACT FILE

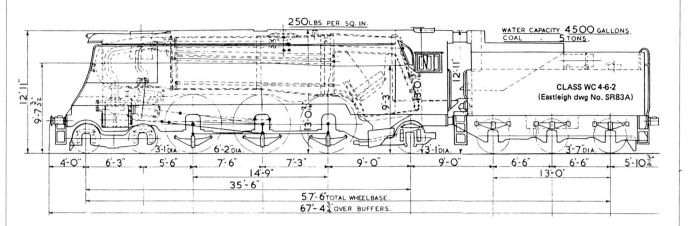

Locomotive Build Details

Build order	2561 (28th Sept 1944)
Where built	Brighton Works (SR)
Date delivered	April 1946
First shed	Ramsgate
Running number	21C127
Date renumbered	July 1948
New BR running number	34027
Date repainted	December 1951
V-cab fitted	June 1953
Date rebuilt	September 1957
Place of rebuild	Eastleigh
Rebuild order number	HO8428
Last shed	Brighton
Date withdrawn	August 1964
Mileage (unrebuilt)	505,083
Mileage (rebuilt)	261,231
Disposal	Woodham Bros., Barry

Dimensions/Data (as running, July 1993)

Overall length	67 ft 4 in
Width (max)	9 ft 0 in
Height (max)	12 ft 11 in

Wheelbase (loco)
6 ft 3 in + 5 ft 6 in + 7 ft 6 in
+ 7 ft 3 in + 9 ft 0 in .... = 35 ft 6 in
Wheelbase (tender)
6 ft 6 in + 6 ft 6 in .... = 13 ft 0 in
Weight (*working) .... 90 tons 1 cwt (Loco)
.... + 47 tons 16 cwt (Tender)
Total *working weight .... 137 tons 17 cwt

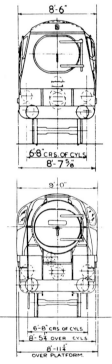

Other Data (as running, July 1993)

Weight distribution:

Bogie	17 tons 8 cwt
Leading coupled axle	19 tons 12 cwt
Centre coupled axle	19 tons 15 cwt
Training coupled axle	18 tons 19 cwt
Trailing truck	14 tons 15 cwt
Tender leading axle	15 tons 16 cwt
Tender centre axle	15 tons 18 cwt
Tender trailing axle	16 tons 2 cwt
Boiler diameter	5 ft 9¾ in to 6 ft 3½ in
Boiler tube length	17 ft 0 in (outer),
	16 ft 9½ in (inner)
Firebox length	6 ft 11 in
Firegrate area	38.25 sq ft
Heating surface	2,610 sq ft
Boiler pressure	250 lb sq in
Cylinders (3)	16⅜ in x 24 in
Piston valves	10 in (outside admission)
Tractive effort	27,715 lb force
	(85% boiler pressure)
Valve gear	Walschaerts (3 independent sets)
Coupled wheel diameter	6 ft 2 in
	(Bulleid/Firth/Brown patent type)
Bogie wheel diameter	3 ft 1 in
Trailing wheel diameter	3 ft 1 in
Tender (T3254) Coal	6.5 tons with extension
Tender water	5500 Gallons
Tender wheel dia	3 ft 7 in

(T3254 on 34027 has ex-Class 47 wheel sets
and ex-LNER axleboxes and spring hangers)

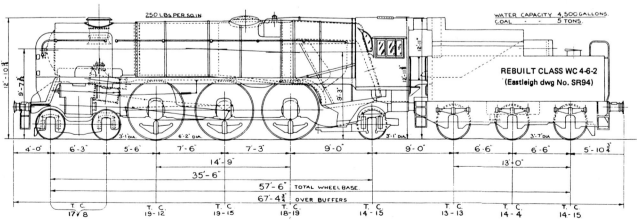

'Working' taken as 145lb/sq in boiler pressure, light fire, 3in water; tender tank full with 5,500 gallons, 6.5 tons coal, drawbar tight.

Chapter One

TAW VALLEY IN SOUTHERN RAILWAY AND BR SERVICE 1946-1964

Taw Valley is one of 110 'West Country' and 'Battle of Britain' class locomotives designed by O.V.S. Bulleid for the Southern Railway. The locomotive was built in 1946 at Brighton and numbered 21C127. She was originally built with a unique design of chain driven valve gear enclosed within an oil bath and air smoothed casing over the boiler and smokebox. These proved to be extremely troublesome, and the class in general, although noted for their power and free running capabilities, were prone to violent bouts of slipping and even bursting into flames as oil-soaked boiler cladding ignited from the sparks. On completion, 21C127 tipped the scales at 128 tons 10 cwt. Until mid-1948 21C127 was used mainly on commuter services on the North Kent coast whilst shedded at Ramsgate. She was then transferred as British Railway's 34027 to Exmouth Junction, the S.R. shed for Exeter and the South West.

The original Light Pacifics, as they were also known, developed many faults. In 1956 it was decided to rebuild the class on more conventional lines. 34027 was in the works at Eastleigh for repairs in early 1957 when she was rebuilt at a cost of £9803.00; a fraction of the cost required to restore her to the standard you see today. Gone was the Bulleid chain-driven valve gear and the air smoothed casing and in its place three sets of Walschaerts valve gear and a conventional boiler outline with large smoke deflectors. The appearance of the rebuilt engines very much resembled that of the BR Standard Pacifics built to R.A.Riddle's designs, in the early 1950's.

Upon completion she was reallocated to Ramsgate for 18 months, then Bricklayer's Arms where, until 1961, she worked a variety of routes including the Cuckoo line to Eastbourne, the Lavender line to Brighton and the Bluebell line via East Grinstead and Haywards Heath. From 1961 she was based at Brighton, a depot with few duties for such a large locomotive and in November 1963 she was put in store as surplus to requirements only to be restored to active duty the following spring. Actual withdrawal followed in August 1964, a mere seven years after rebuilding, with only 764,316 miles to her credit. She was sold to Woodham's Scrap Yard in Barry, South Wales, where she remained until 1980.

Below: **Built at Brighton in 1946, the still unnamed 21C127 stands at Ashford with a Ramsgate bound train on 19th August 1947. Note the superb gantry of semaphore signals and the two men in khaki uniform, presumably on National Service, in the brake.**
Les Elsey.

Top: **Now in British Railways ownership and named but still with high sided tender and slit front cab windows *Taw Valley* was at Eastleigh on 19th December 1951.** Les Elsey.

Above: **At Battledown Flyover just south of Basing stoke. *Taw Valley* hauls an up West of England express on 8th September 1952. Both *Taw Valley* and the photographer are still going strong but only the locomotive has been rebuilt!** Brian Morrison.

Left: **21C127 stands on Exmouth Junction Shed, in the late 1940's.** J.Stirrup collection.

Top left: **In the West of England *Taw Valley*
enters Launceston with two coaches and
what appears to be a single wagon on 3rd
September 1953. A wealth of detail is
available of the old LSWR layout.** S.C.Nash.

Top right: **Working with a clear exhaust on
a Waterloo-West of England express, *Taw
Valley*, now with raked front cab windows,
climbs Honiton Bank in 1954.**
Brian Marshall.

Above: **In more or less the same position as
the earlier SR photograph, *Taw Valley*
stands in company with an S15 at Exmouth
Junction shed., in the early 1950's.**
R.K.Blencowe collection.

Top: *Taw Valley* has charge of a mixed rake of stock on duty No. 467, a Charing Cross to Folkestone service, circa 1958/59. The Stephenson Locomotive Society.

Above left: After rebuilding, *Taw Valley* is seen at the unrebuilt Sevenoaks Station on a service to Folkestone and Dover. The Stephenson Locomotive Society.

Above: *Taw Valley* leaves Salisbury with an 'up' West of England express, before rebuilding. R.K.Blencowe collection.

Above: *Taw Valley* passes Ashford Works with a mixed rake of coaching stock in 1959. R.K.Blencowe collection.

Left: *Taw Valley* stands at Deal with a train for Ramsgate on 31st October 1959. Joanes Publications, Barnstable.

Below left & bottom left : **Two very interesting, if poor quality, shots of *Taw Valley* being prepared and then leaving Eastleigh Yards with a freight train, circa 1960. Author's collection.**

Bottom right: *Taw Valley* stands on Stewarts Lane shed, 27th July 1960. R.K.Blencowe collection.

Left: *Taw Valley* arrives at Exeter Central with a 'down' West of England service, circa 1960-61. Note the AWS piping and contact shoe underneath the front bogie. From the records, *Taw Valley* was fitted with AWS and it was fully functional at this time, but where is the battery box? Historical Model Railway Society.

Below: *Taw Valley* stands at Brighton with a Brighton-Cardiff service. Note the damage to the footplate and the AWS but still no battery box! 22nd September 1962. Robin Lush.

Bottom: Taken as a rear three-quarter view, the young fireman of *Taw Valley* awaits the 'right away' for all points to Salisbury and Cardiff. Note the Standard Class 4 2-6-4 tank coming off the shed and the rich variety of pre-grouping locomotives on the shed, 22nd September 1962. Robin Lush.

Top: **Towards the end of her BR career,** *Taw Valley* **is seen at Polegate on the 08.16 Eastbourne-Hailsham, and** Below, **on the return 0844 working on 31st May 1963.** S.C.Nash.

Chapter Two

BARRY SCRAPYARD AND RESCUE

Above: **The picture that started it all. From the top of 34027 *Taw Valley* the desolate scene of Woodham's scrap yard can be seen. The rows of rusting hulks include a Hughes-Fowler 'Crab' and two ex-BR diesel hydraulic locomotives – D601 *Ark Royal* and D6322. I wonder what the preservationists of today's motive power would give to see D601 and 50035 working together?** Bert Hitchen.

Bottom left: **Bert Hitchen sits on the edge of the smokebox of *Taw Valley* after paying for the locomotive. The hard work was to come.** Liz Hitchen.

Bottom right: **But what a result. Sitting again on the front of *Taw Valley* – this time after breaking the British Rail imposed 'third rail ban', with an excursion that utilised 'unusual motive power' from Ashford to London Bridge. That day – 7th June 1992 – will be remembered for a long time to come, especially by the steam starved Southerners.**

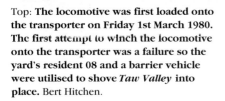

Top: **The locomotive was first loaded onto the transporter on Friday 1st March 1980. The first attempt to winch the locomotive onto the transporter was a failure so the yard's resident 08 and a barrier vehicle were utilised to shove *Taw Valley* into place.** Bert Hitchen.

Above left: **Once in position, rails were laid from the transporter to the track itself. The locomotive was then winched, and pushed by the 08, up onto the back of the low loader.** Bert Hitchen.

Above right: **Once on the low loader the tractor unit was repositioned on the front, the locomotive chained down to prevent** any movement and requisite 'long vehicle' warning boards were positioned for the trip to the locomotive's new home on the North Yorkshire Moors Railway. The work was completed a long time after dark and in this flash assisted shot the contents of the smoke box can be seen, including the superheater tubes, the main steam pipes and the chimney cowlings. Bert Hitchen.

Sequence of three photographs below: In order to lighten or redistribute the weight, the front end of the locomotive was jacked up high enough to allow removal of the bogie. It was done whilst the locomotive was still standing on the trailer! Once the front bogie had been removed the locomotive was repositioned and resecured. The whole rig was then taken out onto the road to see how things looked on the level. It soon became apparent that the tractor and trailer were not up to the job of transporting such a heavy locomotive as far as North Yorkshire. It was, therefore, arranged to unload the locomotive back onto the tracks in the scrapyard until a far heavier 'rig' could be acquired. The weather during the day had turned from snow into cold sleet and the ground had become a quagmire. Towards the end of the day however, the sun finally broke through as *Taw Valley* was slowly hauled backwards onto *terra firma*.
Bert Hitchen.

Above: As already mentioned, the loading was completed very late on the Friday and the whole ensemble had to await until the following day to attempt the trip to the NYMR. Bert and the NYMR team had meanwhile returned home overnight by car. After leaving Barry Docks the next day, the police had stopped the transporter and refused to allow it to continue. The weather conditions of heavy snow and the sheer weight of the load were too much to allow passage. The transporter had already had one puncture and with the deteriorating weather conditions the police requested that the load be redistributed or lightened. So, not withstanding the fact that Bert had just returned home, he had to raise a second team to go back to Barry and sort the mess out. Bert and his team arrived back early on the Sunday morning to find the transporter parked in the entrance to Barry Eastern Docks. After raising the transporter crew and arranging for them to return the locomotive to where it was loaded, Bert and his team went to get some breakfast at a nearby cafe. Upon returning to the loading point the locomotive and transporter were nowhere in sight. When they were eventually located the whole load was in a very precarious situation indeed. The driver in his attempts to get the transporter into the unloading area had swung off the tarmac road and sunk up to the axles in mud! Fortunately there was a heavy plant machinery depot doing some Sunday repair work to their vehicles and they were co-opted to pull the whole rig out of the mud. Bert Hitchen.

Left and below: **As the bogie had been removed from the main body of the locomotive, it was liberally daubed with 'do not cut' reminders. This was to disuade the ever voracious appetite of Woodham's men from cutting up what would appear to them as just another set of wheels. A fresh attempt was made with a rig that far exceeded the requirements of *Taw Valley*. However, a late start and the requirement to replace the front bogie meant a finish using car headlights to illuminate the scene. The trailer finally left Barry on 18th April 1980, and the load was transported slowly northwards, resting overnight at Hartshead services on the M62.** Bert Hitchen.

Bottom left: **At the time of rescue, no genuine Southern tenders were available for purchase. Thus an ex-BR tender was acquired with the idea of rebuilding this into an acceptable accompaniment for the engine. It was transported to the NYMR on 15th February 1980.** Bert Hitchen.

Bottom right: **The locomotive was finally delivered to Pickering on 21st April 1980 from where it was towed to Grosmont by the NYMR's Class 24 diesel.** Bert Hitchen.

Colour Section

TAW VALLEY IN COLOUR

34027 seems to have avoided photographers whose cameras were loaded with colour film. To introduce this brief colour survey of *Taw Valley's* preservation career we are pleased to be able to publish what may well be the only colour pictures taken of the locomotive prior to its withdrawal from service with British Railways.

Top: **What the pictures on this page lack in terms of quality, they make up for in rarity value. In August 1961 *Taw Valley* heads a Bath to Brighton train near Angmering.** The late J.P.Mullett / Colour Rail.

Middle: **Possibly the last photograph taken of *Taw Valley* before withdrawal. The filthy locomotive backs down onto Basingstoke shed on 28th June 1964.** Author's collection.

Bottom: ***Taw Valley* passes near Romsey whilst hauling a Cardiff to Brighton express on 24th April 1962.** Les Elsey.

Top: *Taw Valley* stands as a rusting hulk shortly after purchase. February 1980. Bert Hitchen.

Middle: *Taw Valley* pauses at Hampton Loade on the Severn Valley Railway, after its first test run from Bridgnorth, 25th September 1987. Roger Scanlon.

Bottom: **With full *Golden Arrow* regalia *Taw Valley* stands at the exit to Bridgnorth** shed in readiness to work a special over the SVR, 29th August 1992. Hubert Fingerle

Opposite page top: *Taw Valley* returns the special from Bridgnorth to Kidderminster past Hampton Loade on 29th August 1992. Hubert Fingerle.

Opposite page bottom: *Taw Valley* leaves Kidderminster for Bridgnorth on 17th September 1988.

Above: *Taw Valley* **rests at Holyhead at the head of the *North Wales Coast Express*, August 1990.** Alan Strange.

Below: *Taw Valley* **has reached Newport (Gwent) on its run from Swindon to Hereford, 29th November 1991.** Alan Strange.

Above: *Taw Valley* at East Wimbledon, 5th May 1991.

Below: *Taw Valley* and D400 stand side by side at East Wimbledon, Saturday 5th May 1991.

Above: *Taw Valley* stands at Yeovil Junction with the first Andover-Exeter Central working, Sunday 21st June 1992.

Bottom: 34027 *Taw Valley* disguised as 34028 *Eddystone* at Ashford on Sunday 7th June 1992.

Top left: *Taw Valley* crosses the harbour at Folkestone with one of the *'Harbour Master'* specials, Thursday 12th June 1991.

Top right: **The evening sun catches** *Taw Valley* **as she crosses the viaduct over Folkestone Harbour on Friday 13th June 1991.**

Bottom: *Taw Valley* **and** 777 *Sir Lamiel* **stand in the early Summer sun in Eastleigh Works Yard, 20th June 1992.**

Top: **80080**, **777 *Sir Lamiel***, **70000 *Britannia*** and **34027 *Taw Valley*** stand at Lover's Walk Brighton, 21st September 1991.

Bottom left: *Taw Valley* stands in Platform 14 at Waterloo station, taking water before departure to Bournemouth. The sight of homebound commuters staring in disbelief at the gleaming machine was something to be savoured. I wonder how many commuters when arriving home late after watching the departure said, 'Sorry I'm late dear, I've been watching a steam engine leaving Waterloo' only to be scolded 'You've been watching a steam beer in the bar more likely!' Friday 11th September 1992.

Bottom right: *Taw Valley* was hauled complete with train into Waterloo in the late afternoon prior to the evening departure for Bournemouth. Here *Taw Valley* stands at the head of the train awaiting departure from Platform 8, Friday 11th September 1992.

Chapter Three

RESTORATION

Below: **As very little progress was being made on the project at the NYMR the decision was taken to move the locomotive to the East Lancashire Railway at Bury. The engine eventually arrived in November 1982. Once at Bury, work progressed at a more favourable pace. Here the bolts holding the smokebox to its saddle are being removed by oxy-acetylene torch. The exhaust pipe from the cylinder can clearly be seen as can the two holes for the main steam pipes to this outside cylinder and** the inside cylinder (right and left respectively). Bert Hitchen.

Below right: **The bolts holding the regulator valve and actuating linkage assembly are here being removed. The cladding on the cab had been taken away leaving the bare framework on which to rebuild. Bert Hitchen.**

Bottom right: **This view inside the partially dismantled smokebox shows the tube plate** complete with the main flue tubes, (32 in number), and most of the associated small tubes. Also seen is the superheater header with the three joints for the main steam pipes to the cylinders, and superheater pipe joints underneath, the chimney petticoat and the Le-Maitre multiple jet blast pipe. The protruberance on the bottom left of the tube plate is a superheater element that was jammed in a collapsed main flue tube. Perhaps this was the reason for withdrawal? Bert Hitchen.

Above & below left: **The boiler was lifted in March 1983. The wheels were removed the same day by using the boiler lift crane. Here the ELR staff take the three sets of 6ft. 2in. main driving wheels and axle boxes out of the frames. Close examination of the frames shows the brake hangers, the horn guides, the main pin holding the front bogie in place and various other details useful especially to modellers. The locomotive had by now acquired a new set of buffers.** Bert Hitchen.

Bottom right: **The tender acquired from Barry for *Taw Valley* was never taken to the ELR. It was now to be utilised as the tender for the ex-BR Class 4 4-6-0 75014, now resident on the NYMR. Instead, a brand new Bulleid pattern tender tank was constructed by Shipyard Services of Brightlingsea Essex, using Lloyds Grade A shipbuilding steel. The body was then transported to Riley & Son (Electromec) Ltd. of Heywood, Lancashire, where the underframe was fabricated and wheels and axleboxes fitted. The wheels, axleboxes and springing gear were from an ex-LNER tender chassis. Delivery to the East Lancs Railway was on 20th December 1983.** Bert Hitchen.

Sequence of photographs on this page:
Owing to contractual difficulties with the ELR, after the majority of the rebuilding work had been completed, it was arranged that the locomotive and tender were to be moved to the Severn Valley Railway. The reassembly of the locomotive, for transport and loading purposes only, was undertaken outside the main workshops of the ELR. Two hydraulic cranes were utilised to lift the already completed chassis onto a low loader. From this position the boiler was replaced on the frames and secured.
Bert Hitchen.

Top: **After leaving the ELR the locomotive arrived at the Severn Valley Railway in November 1985. The locomotive was berthed in the car park at Bridgnorth station before unloading in the shed yard.** Bert Hitchen.

Above left: **Even though the locomotive looked in near complete condition when it arrived at Bridgnorth, plenty of work was still required to complete the job. Alan Schofield uses an air gun to caulk stays on the firebox. Note the ear defenders which are a must when doing a job like this.** Bert Hitchen.

Above right: **The two outside main steam pipes are in position and it only remains to fit the centre or middle cylinder steam pipe. Alan Schofield sits on the blastpipe whilst working inside the smoke box to fit this pipe. The large diameter chimney cowl with its fitting bolts for the spark arrester can be seen.** Bert Hitchen.

Top: **From a vantage point on the top of the boiler of an adjacent locomotive the unclad boiler of *Taw Valley* can be seen. The main steam pipe is that running along the firebox to the main steam manifold cut off valve, lying beside the dome on the driver's side of the boiler. The skeleton for the cladding is already taking shape on the firebox side. The mass of small bore lubricating pipes is also well displayed running between the footplating and the cab corner. October 1986.** Bert Hitchen.

Bottom left: **In more congenial weather, four of the crew who were working on the locomotive pose for a 'family photo'. The wrinkle in the smoke box door can be seen; it's still there to this day. From left to right are, Bert Hitchen, Alan Schofield, Steve Jennings and Ken Kitchen.** Liz Hitchen.

Middle: **When the locomotive was ready for steam testing the whole unit was towed outside into the yard at Bridgnorth for steam to be raised for the first time since 1964. The date is April 1987.** Bert Hitchen.

Below left: **The boiler was hydraulically tested in March 1987 to check for leaks from the riveting and associated pipe work and to check the action of the thermic syphons. During the last week in April 1987, for the first time in 23 years the boiler begins to produce steam. The blanking plates for the regulator housing and the unclad boiler contrast with the state of today.** Bert Hitchen.

Below right: **At long last the day arrived when steam was to be raised for the first time. The SVR's Sambron fills the tender with best Bridgnorth coal. April 1987.** Bert Hitchen.

Bottom: **The first loaded test run of the nearly completed locomotive was behind locomotive 80079 to Hampton Loade. At the station _Taw Valley_ was taken off and** allowed to return to Bridgnorth under her own steam. With all the boiler cladding now in place but not yet painted and with her original tender and wheels – note the spokes – _Taw Valley_ stands on the down line at Hampton Loade awaiting a final inspection before proceeding back to Bridgnorth. The date was mid-September 1987. Bert Hitchen.

Chapter Four

SEVERN VALLEY DAYS

Left: **The smoke deflectors were fitted on 26th September 1987 and further running in turns, including some 'Santa Specials', with the almost completed locomotive were undertaken. With the starting signal 'off',** *Taw Valley* **awaits the 'right away' from the guard, with a train at Bridgnorth during October.** Bert Hitchen.

Below: *Taw Valley* **stands at the buffer stops at Kidderminster (SVR) Station after arriving with a test train. The locomotive stands complete with a 72B shed plate. She lacks electric lights and a dome cover and is still in light grey undercoat when this picture was taken in October 1987.** Bert Hitchen.

Above: **The locomotive entered the SVR paintshops in late February 1988. After completion a resplendent *Taw Valley* stands at the signals on the approach to Bridgnorth in the late evening sun on 4th June 1988. Once again the original tender with spoked wheels and original coal capacity can be seen. The quality of the workmanship of the SVR painters is a major factor in the continuing well turned out appearance that *Taw Valley* has whenever the locomotive goes onto the main line or other preserved railways.** Roger Scanlon.

Centre right: **The locomotive was bought for Liz as a birthday present, being paid for on that day in January 1980. Here, after all the work had been completed and the locomotive passed fit for service, Bert gives Liz a single rose at the naming ceremony at Kidderminster Town Station on 4th June 1988.**

Below: ***Taw Valley* leaves Kidderminster under the still to be completed gantry controlling the entrance to the new station on Saturday 17th September 1988. The use of a traditional oil lamp seems somewhat**

anachronistic considering the locomotive is equipped with electric lighting.

Above: The beautiful Great Western signal box at the SVR station in Kidderminster, which looks like a treasured relic from the age of steam, was in fact built in the 1980s to control the brand new station. The SVR's Kidderminster Town station must rank as one of the finest achievements of the railway preservation movement in Britain.

Above right: This time with the electric lights piercing the gloom of an English summer's day, *Taw Valley* climbs towards Bewdley Tunnel with an afternoon service.

Below: The locomotive has spent a considerable amount of time away from the SVR on various main line workings and visits to other preserved steam railways. However, the locomotive made a welcome return in late summer 1992. On a very wet Saturday 22nd August, *Taw Valley* climbs away from Bewdley for Kidderminster.

Left: *Taw Valley* was in service all through the Christmas period of 1988. Santa waves from the cab of the locomotive whilst it is standing at Arley waiting to take a service back to Kidderminster. The steam generator is situated beneath the cab on this, the driver's side. The vacuum ejector can be seen through the angled window. The tunnel in which the fire irons are stored can be seen beneath the tender cab window.

Below: No visit to the SVR can be complete without a photograph of John Fowler's famous cast iron bridge over the River Severn. *Taw Valley* proceeds towards Arley on Saturday 22nd August 1992.

Top right: *Taw Valley* climbs out of Bridgnorth towards Oldbury Viaduct and Daniel's Mill. Southern Railway type discs are in use on this service in lieu of the electric lights on Saturday 22nd August 1992.

Centre: *Taw Valley* in the shed yard at Bridgnorth in the early Spring of 1989 is about to be coaled in preparation for another days work on the 'Valley'

Below: *Taw Valley* in service on the SVR performed its tasks with effortless ease and surprising economy. Even staunch GWR men were soon converted to this 'foreign' locomotive. Rumours soon spread that a plan to fire the locomotive with only a bank of candles just under the firehole door was being given serious consideration since it steamed so well! The locomotive is being cleaned on Bridgnorth shed ready for a day's duty on Saturday 17th September 1988.

Chapter Five

RETURN TO THE MAIN LINE

THE WELSH MARCHES

Left: *Taw Valley* eventually made her main line test trip on Thursday 11th May 1989. The route was the standard one from Derby via the Erewash Valley line to Sheffield and return was undertaken in miserable weather. Here *Taw Valley* is seen on the four track section of the Erewash Valley line. Author's collection.

Below: The first main line outing for *Taw Valley* was on the 'West Mercian'. Here *Taw Valley* passes Crewe Gresty Lane No.1 Box with the outward train on Saturday 20th May 1989. Tony Moseley.

Right: **After working to Hereford the locomotive was coaled and watered then turned on the triangle at Bulmer's Railway Centre ready for the return to Crewe.** *Taw Valley* **stands on the through road during the 'photo stop' at Shrewsbury on Saturday 20th May 1989. This was hardly conducive to good customer relations, especially to those on the train!**

Below: **After working on Network SouthEast during the late Summer/Autumn of 1991 the locomotive returned via Hereford to Crewe in order to take up its Winter schedule on the Settle & Carlisle Line. Here the locomotive awaits to work the positioning special from Swindon to Hereford, Friday 29th November 1991.** John Stretton.

Bottom: **After visiting the Keighley & Worth Valley Railway during the early part of 1992,** *Taw Valley* **proceeds with a support coach to Crewe, to haul a** *Welsh Marches Express* **from Crewe to Hereford. The locomotive stands at Northwich during a lay-over on Friday 24th April 1992.**

HEADING SOUTH

Right: **The locomotive used to return the**
***Welsh Marches Express* to Crewe was**
John Cameron's A4 Pacific 60009 *Union of*
***South Africa*. *Taw Valley* stands on the line**
connecting the Bulmer's Railway Centre to
the main line whilst 60009 awaits the
passage of a Class 37 hauled freight, before
backing down to the station to pick up the
train, on Saturday 25th April 1992.

Centre right: ***Taw Valley* at Worcester on**
Thursday 10th September 1992 on its way
South for further duties, after its stint on
the SVR.

Below left: ***Taw Valley* stands at Evesham**
station awaiting a path over the single line
to Honeybourne and Moreton-in-Marsh.
For an unadvertised light engine working,
this movement certainly had its fair share
of onlookers! Also photographed on
Thursday 10th September 1992.

Below right: **The locomotive then**
proceeded to Didcot where coal and water
were taken. In the late evening, *Taw Valley*,
under its own power, was taken to
Wimbledon Depot to await the following
day's exertions. Here *Taw Valley* stands in
company with the fine Didcot collection of
GWR locomotives, including 5029 *Nunney*
Castle* and the superbly restored 6024 *King
***Edward I*. Later still, on Thursday 10th**
September 1992.

THE NORTH WALES COAST EXPRESS

Left: **In June 1989 *Taw Valley* was one of the locomotives given the honour of taking part in the inaugural year of the *North Wales Coast Express* workings from Crewe to Holyhead and return. Here she awaits 'the off' on platform 12 at Crewe Station on 20th June 1989.** Brian Cooke.

Below left: **As with all plans of mice and men, things do not always go as planned. *Clan Line* had been sent ahead to Holyhead to power the return working. However, at Prestatyn, all was not well with *Taw Valley*. The trouble was traced to a seized valve spindle. *Clan Line* was quickly recalled from Holyhead to Llandudno Junction** where the errant *Taw Valley* was removed from the train. *Clan Line* then worked the remainder of the outward trip and the return without further mishap. Here we see both Bulleids side by side at the junction on 20th June 1989. K.J.C.Jackson.

Below right: **Once repaired, *Taw Valley* continued to give sterling service throughout the summer. Here the locomotive stands in Bangor Station on a return working, on 16th July 1989.** K.J.C.Jackson.

Bottom: ***Taw Valley* looks like a model as she passes under the footbridge leading into Chester station. Bert Hitchen leans out of the support coach. The tender is well supplied with coal for the 200 or so mile trip. There were journeys when *Taw Valley* needed every bit of coal in the tender!**

Above: *Taw Valley* is well into her stride as the locomotive passes the semaphore signals protecting Abergele Station on a brilliant summer's day in 1990. Steve Kirk.

Above: **From the junction the whole train was taken up the branch to Llandudno itself. Here** *Taw Valley* **arrives on an overcast day in 1990.** Steve Kirk.

Bottom: *Taw Valley* **brings a weekday service into Llandudno junction in 1990.** Steve Kirk.

Top left: **After arrival at Holyhead the locomotive draws forward to be prepared for the light engine trip to Valley in order to turn on the triangle especially built for these steam specials. Behind** *Taw Valley* **can be seen one of the Irish ferry boats at its moorings next to the station. The harbour at Holyhead was developed by the London & North Western Railway specifically for the Irish traffic. August 1990.**

Top right: **The climb out of Holyhead is very steep but the crews soon got the hang of handling the Pacific locomotive across the pointwork and up the bank. Here** *Taw Valley* **climbs away on a sunny summer's day in 1990. The tender coal spray is being used to dampen down the dust, the safety valves are about to blow and the clear exhaust of the Bulleid shows the engine to be working hard on the climb. Steve Kirk.**

Second down: **Eastbound for Llandudno Junction, Chester and Crewe, we see** *Taw Valley* **passing Conway on 1st August 1990.** K.J.C.Jackson.

Bottom: **After leaving Colwyn Bay Station the railway skirts the sea before passing over the A55. Here** *Taw Valley* **crosses the main coast road under very light steam in August 1990.** K.J.C.Jackson.

THE NORTH WALES COAST EXPRESS

Left: **From the old freight sidings at Rhyl** *Taw Valley* **restarts the train as the sun begins to drop into eventide. The remains of the once crowded signal gantry stands out stark against the early evening sky in this August 1990 view.** Steve Kirk.

Second down: **Saltney Junction is now but a shadow of its former self with only two tracks remaining. Here** *Taw Valley* **speeds the 11 coach formation towards Chester's ancient city walls. August 1990.**

Third down: **The old Chester (LMS) shed was situated where the new estate, seen here above the locomotive, now stands. After the reverse curves of Chester station and the pointwork,** *Taw Valley* **is working hard to lift the 11 coaches weighing some 400 tons away to Crewe. The popularity of the service fell off after the first two years due mainly to its midweek timing, lack of publicity and state of the coaching stock.**

Below: **On the return working, 1st August 1990,** *Taw Valley* **was almost out of coal by the time Chester was reached. From Chester the locomotive was nursed as far as Crewe Heritage Centre where it was stopped. The boiler pressure was so low that sufficient vacuum could not be obtained to blow off the brakes. The station pilot, a Class 08 shunter, was sent to assist. After coupling up the 08 failed to get the brakes off and could not manage the train on its own. In the end** *Taw Valley* **had to push the shunter and drag its own train into Crewe Station after raising more steam by burning wood found lying along the trackside.** K.J.C.Jackson.

MARYLEBONE AND SOUTHALL

Below left: **This was during the days of the converted Class 25 Electric Train Heating Locomotives (ETHELs).** *ETHEL 3*, **painted in InterCity livery, is seen here between** *Taw Valley* **and its support coach. This was the first working of a rebuilt Bulleid Light Pacific into London since July 1967. The train was a returning** *South Yorkshireman* **from Derby on Saturday 18th November 1989.**

Below right: *Taw Valley* **rests on the through road of the** *Clan Line* **shed at**

Southall whilst being prepared for a *'Robin Hood'* working to and from Nottingham during late December 1989. The room and the excellent facilities can clearly be seen.

Bottom left: *Taw Valley* on the exit line of the depot passes *Clan Line* on the shed through line on a sunny Friday, 19th January 1990. *Clan Line* was being prepared for its six monthly examination and *Taw Valley* was being made ready for a *'Robin Hood'* the following day. Once again the ex-MN tender can be closely viewed.

Bottom right: **During a later visit to Southall in 1991 the major task of remetalling all the driving axle box bearings was undertaken. To do this the facilities in the**

shed were utilised, whilst *Flying Scotsman* was away working in the North. Here *Taw Valley* stands minus all driving wheels. The SVR engineers came to optically align the frames thus enabling Tom Tighe at Dairycoates (Hull) to correctly remachine the boxes. At the same time all the side rod bushes were remetalled. The wheel drop can be seen under the trailing bogie of *Taw Valley*. (The driving wheels are hardly visible on the extreme right of the picture). Various pieces of motion can also be seen scattered about the floor. All this was done within four weeks: surely a record in preservation for a locomotive away from a private railway! Saturday 6th April 1991.

Left: **On the *'Robin Hood'*, on Saturday 20th January 1990, 34027 passes the photographer and continues on towards Hatton Station and Dorridge, where the next water will be taken. The water coming from the ash pan on the driver's side is from the ash pan dampers, with which all Bulleid Pacifics were fitted. Also note that the tender spray is on, thus damping down any dust from the coal in the tender.**

Below: **After leaving Dorridge, still on Saturday 20th January 1990, the train was routed via Tyseley and St. Andrews curve to Saltley where a crew change occurred. It then travelled to Water Orton and in this case Lea Marston, Kingsbury and on to Tamworth. After taking the left fork at Water Orton East junction and passing over the River Tame *Taw Valley* coasts along towards Kingsbury Junction.**

Bottom: **The train approaches Nottingham under light steam, late on Saturday 20th January 1990.**

Top right: **These pictures record the locomotives last run from Marylebone on Saturday 31st March 1990.** *Taw Valley* **stands at the station on its** *'Robin Hood'* **working to Nottingham. It returned to Saltley from where** *Taw Valley* **was taken off to go back to the SVR. The locomotive had a reduced load of only seven coaches as bookings at this time were considerably down.** K.J.C.Jackson.

Centre left: *Taw Valley* **blasts out of Marylebone for the Chilterns and beyond.** Steve Kirk.

Centre right: **Water was taken at both Banbury and Dorridge.** *Taw Valley* **is seen shortly after leaving Dorridge station heading for Widney Manor and Saltley.**

Bottom: **The day dawned very misty but by the time the train was approaching Saunderton Summit the sun was beginning to burn off that early mist. This is one of my favourite photographs of** *Taw Valley*.

THE SETTLE & CARLISLE LINE

The 'Blue Riband' for any preserved main line steam locomotive is a run over the Settle & Carlisle (S&C) line. For the first few years of *Taw Valley's* preservation life, a run in either direction over the line had been denied. The locomotive was finally given two runs, one in each direction in late December 1991 and early February 1992. A bonus came in the allocation of one of the 'Royal Scotsman' steam legs from Bradford Forster Square to Carlisle on 28th December 1991. Coupled with this was a visit to the Keighley & Worth Valley Railway for the early Spring of 1992.

Top left: **Making a superb exhaust *Taw Valley* powers her way northwards towards Ribblehead with the train. The earlier anxieties of slipping to a standstill at Stainforth Tunnel had come to nothing.** Chris Milner.

Centre left: **The remaining photographs on this page were taken on Saturday 8th February. Here *Taw Valley* gets into its stride after being halted at Culgaith Box.** K.J.C.Jackson.

Bottom left: ***Taw Valley* stands 'under the wires' with a sell out *Cumbrian Mountain Express*. The participants were to be treated to a superb run over the 'Long Drag' spoiled only by a failed distant signal at Kirkby Stephen. The timings to Kirkby were some 6 seconds better than those of 71000 when it took the 'Blue Riband'.**

Below: **Two run pasts were arranged on this trip. This is the only time that the people on the train get to see and photograph the locomotive working. *Taw Valley* with sanders full on passes Appleby North Signal Box and the junction down to North Eastern sidings and the Warcop Branch.**

ON THE K&WVR

Right: **The 1992 southbound CMEs had steam haulage from Carlisle to Farrington Junction. This included the climb from Whalley Viaduct to Whilpshire Tunnel at a ruling gradient of some 1 in 80. After leaving the train at Farrington Junction the locomotive and support coach then travelled back via Blackburn, Hellifield and Skipton to the K&WVR for a short early springtime visit. *Taw Valley* was to be one of the guest attractions at the K&WVR Spring Gala in early April 1992. However the first run over the line occurred a week earlier. Here *Taw Valley* stands alongside the magnificent double chimneyed Jubilee 45596 *Bahamas* at Haworth, on Sunday 29th March 1992.**

Below: **The first movement of the locomotive was a light engine trip to Oxenhope to pick up the coaching stock. Here *Taw Valley* leaves Haworth bound for the terminus on Sunday 29th March 1992.**

Right: ***Taw Valley* climbs away from the industrial heart of Keighley over the Oxenhope Road and towards Ingrow on Sunday 29th March 1992.**

Below: **The other locomotive in action that weekend was the LMS 0-6-0T 47279. After its last train of the day had been returned to Oxenhope the 0-6-0T was coupled up to *Taw Valley* and 48431, which was on a 'running in' turn, to provide the spectacle of a 'triple header' coasting down to Haworth. Super power indeed! Sunday 29th March 1992.**

Chapter Six

BACK TO THE SOUTHERN

LONDON BRIDGE OPEN DAY

Left: On 30th March 1991 *Taw Valley* **attended her first open day at London Bridge, in company with 35028** *Clan Line.* **Here** *Taw Valley* **stands in the early spring sun.** B.R. Civil Engineers, Croydon

EAST WIMBLEDON OPEN DAY

After the remetalling of the main driving wheel axle boxes (see page 43) the first outing for *Taw Valley* was with 35028 *Clan Line* to an open day at Wimbledon East Depot on the weekend of 5th/6th May 1991. The two locomotives travelled via Acton Main Line, Acton Wells Junction, Willesden S.W. Sidings, West London Junction, North Pole Junction, Kensington Olympia and Latchmere Junction to Clapham Junction. Here *Taw Valley* was removed and was sent via Putney, Strawberry Hill, Kingston and Wimbledon to turn. The only way into Wimbledon East Depot from Wimbledon Station is via the carriage wash. *Taw Valley* was duly sent this way and was taken through the wash at a crawl. However just at this time a London Transport bus driver was crossing the road bridge and saw the smoke and steam rising. The driver immediately stopped and summoned the Fire Brigade who promptly arrived only to find that the steam and smoke was from *Taw Valley* and not a conflagration in the washing plant! The two locomotives were used on a shuttle up and down the sidings in the depot. This was the first passenger steam working over the third rail since *Clan Line* took a special from Basingstoke to Westbury in April 1974.

Above: *Taw Valley* stands besides the recently renovated D400 (50050). D400 and 59005 were also used on a shuttle up and down the yard, Saturday 5th May 1991.

Above: **Not the South Western in the late 1950's, but Saturday 5th May 1991, as** *Taw Valley* **hauls the shuttle past the National Railway Museum's 4-SUB at Wimbledon Staff Halt.**

Top left: **Three forms of Southern motive power meet at the Staff Halt.** *Taw Valley* **is on the shuttle, 4-SUB 4732 stands by the depot and Class 50 50049** *Defiance* **passes on an 'up' West of England express on Saturday 5th May 1991.**

Top right: **After dark the two locomotives were positioned behind the main administrative buildings for watering, coaling and maintenance. The sight of two Bulleid Pacifics, both in steam, standing on a Southern depot is something a lot of people, both involved with the locomotives and behind the scenes, had worked very hard for a long time to see. Sunday 6th May 1991.**

Right: *Clan Line* **pulls the shuttle past the Staff Halt and the 4-SUB as Bert Hitchen leans out of the cab of** *Taw Valley*.

Bottom right: **The weekend did not pass without its share of mishaps. On the way into the depot an object jammed behind the trailing wheel of the bogie on the driver's side. This caused the wheel to slide and produced a bad flat on the tyre, noticeable when travelling on the footplate, by a bad knock. The only cure was to put the locomotive onto the wheel lathe at the depot and turn the tyre down thus removing the flat. Here** *Taw Valley* **moves slowly onto the lathe which, up to that time, had only seen class 455 units and the like. Sunday 6th May 1991.**

THE NETWORK HARBOUR MASTERS

The first two weeks in September 1991 had *Taw Valley* working almost continuously. The locomotive together with ex-BR Standard Class 4 Tank No 80080 was chosen to work a series of shuttles over the third rail electrified branch from Folkestone Harbour to Folkestone Junction as part of the Shepway Festival. *Taw Valley* at the beginning of the month was working on the NYMR. From here the locomotive travelled light engine with its support coach to York where it was stabled overnight at the NRM. The next day the engine worked a positioning special from Sheffield to Didcot and thence to Southall. After servicing over the weekend, *Taw Valley*, 80080 and their support vehicles travelled overnight and over the third rail to Ashford's Chart Leacon Depot. The only locomotives to be seen in steam on BR in the 'Garden of England' since the end of steam had been 35028 *Clan Line* on test in the 1970's and 34072 *257 Squadron* at its renaming and dedication ceremony at Folkestone the previous year. This was to be different as passengers were to be hauled. The services showed a 70% loading and a sizeable donation made to charity at the end. These two days demonstrated that using steam power on certain services could generate considerable income both for Network SouthEast and the local traders. 80080 and *Taw Valley* parted company at Hither Green on the return. 80080 went on to Southall as she made her way to South Wales to work specials in the Valleys. *Taw Valley* continued on to appear in the open day at Cambridge Station on Saturday 14th September 1991.

Top: **After the open day at Wimbledon the locomotive was worked light engine to Derby for weighing and resetting of the springs. From there it was worked back to the NYMR for the early summer season. Here** *Taw Valley* **begins the climb out of the Esk Valley for Goathland and Pickering on 25th August 1991.**

Centre: **Remnants of the old order are still to be found at Battersby on the Whitby to Middlesborough line. Here** *Taw Valley* **runs around by the old 'NER 1907' water column on Thursday 5th September 1991.**

Bottom: *Taw Valley* **stands under the noon-day sun on the centre road of Sheffield Midland Station on Friday 6th September 1991. Though still a long way from its home territory it already sports 'The Man of Kent' headboard.**

Right: **From a vantage point on the walkway around the depot building at Ashford, *Taw Valley* awaits coaling on Wednesday 11th September 1991. John Dale stands in the enlarged coal space.**

Centre: **The test train comprised Class 33 33211, *Taw Valley*, the two support coaches, a rake of 'grampus' wagons and 80080 in the rear as it prepares to leave Ashford on Wednesday 11th September 1991.**

Bottom: **The honour of being the first locomotive down to the harbour was given to 80080 on a light engine gauging run. The test train proper was formed of *Taw Valley*, the two support coaches, the rake of 'grampus' wagons, with 80080 and 33211 in the rear in case assistance was required. The train is seen here awaiting the first trial trip from the Harbour. Steve McColl, on the track, discusses the day's proceedings with Inspector Derek Bourne, Wednesday 11th September 1991 again.**

Above: **This superb night shot of *Taw Valley* and 80080 in the head-shunt at Chart Leacon typifies the condition that the support crews kept the locomotives during the Folkestone Harbour trips.**

Centre: **The Pacific's *'The Man Of Kent'* headboard, was an original. Here *Taw Valley* and 80080 await the off on a sunny Thursday, 12th September 1991.**

Bottom: **The two support coaches were taken down by diesel to Folkestone Junction whilst the train proper was marshalled in the yard at Ashford. The whole train was 'piloted' by freshly outshopped Class 73 73126 *Kent & East Sussex Railway*. 73126 stood by as spare engine. Here the train arrives at the junction from Ashford on Thursday 12th September 1991.**

Top left: **Photographed from the roof of a prominent hotel, *Taw Valley* crosses the swing bridge over the harbour as it climbs away with an afternoon service on Thursday 12th September 1991.**

Top right: **The first train on 12th September arrives at the top of the climb. The gradient of 1 in 30 can be appreciated from the angle of *Taw Valley's* train in relation to the main line in the foreground.**

Bottom: **A classic SR scene is recreated as *Taw Valley* crosses the harbour bridge and gets down to tackling the gradient up to the junction on Thursday 12th September 1991.**

Above: **After the shuttles had finished the locomotives and support coaches were dispatched to Dover to be watered and turned for the trip back to London. Another classic SR scene is re-enacted, for the first time since the demise of steam on the *'Golden Arrow'* in June 1961, when 34100 *Appledore* was the motive power. *Taw Valley* and 80080 stand in platform 4 at Dover Western Docks on Friday 13th September 1991.**

Left: **The work force at Chart Leacon gathered with the support crews for this 'family photo' at the depot. The staff of Chart Leacon gave us a lot of help and assistance during our stay at the depot with special thanks going to Mr Alan Crotty. Friday 13th September 1991.**

BRIGHTON OPEN DAY

After an appearance at the open day at Cambridge, *Taw Valley* together with 70000 Britannia returned to Southall. From Southall four locomotives were invited to attend the open day at Brighton Lover's Walk depot. The locomotives were 777 *Sir Lamiel*, 80080, 70000 *Britannia* and 34027 *Taw Valley*. The ensemble left Southall on Friday 20th September and was piloted by a Class 33 to Brighton. *Taw Valley* was to be the first locomotive into Brighton Station in steam since the end of steam running. This was for the naming of a Class 73 73128 *O.V.S. Bulleid C.B.E.* after the last Chief Mechanical Engineer of the Southern Railway, on Saturday 21st September 1992. After the open day the four locomotives all in steam but still piloted were returned via East Croydon to Southall.

Top right: **80080, 777, 70000 and *Taw Valley* stand on display at Lover's Walk on Saturday 21st September 1991.**

Middle right: ***Taw Valley* hauls the newly named Class 73 73128 *O.V.S. Bulleid C.B.E., C.M.E. Southern Railway, 1937-1949,* into Brighton Lover's Walk Depot. 73128 together with the Pullman-liveried 73101 hauled the Venice Simplon Orient Express Pullman set to and from London Victoria during the weekend. Saturday 21st September 1991 again.**

Bottom: **This night shot shows the four locomotives together with the former London, Brighton & South Coast Railway. 0-4-2 No.214 *Gladstone*. The Jubilee and ex-LBSCR Class A1X 0-6-0T No. 55 *Stepney* were on loan from the National Collection and the Bluebell Railway respectively for the open day, Sunday 22nd September 1991.**

CAMBRIDGE – KING'S LYNN

Following the success of the open day at Cambridge a series of steam hauled specials were instigated from Cambridge to King's Lynn. This was the final opportunity to use steam on the 'Fen Line' as 25Kv overhead wires were to be energised shortly after the weekend. Three locomotives were utilised, 4472 *Flying Scotsman*, 70000 *Britannia* and *Taw Valley*. Both 4472 and 70000 had seen service through Cambridge during their respective LNER and BR careers. *Taw Valley* was a 'foreign' engine being 'Southern' based but with its tender being fitted for tender first running it was considered an ideal partner for the other two. Two locomotives were set facing King's Lynn, 70000 and 34027, whilst 4472 was positioned facing Cambridge. At certain times during the weekend two engines would be on the road together thus giving the spectacle of two steam hauled express passenger trains passing one another at some point. This weekend was the final time that steam power was to be seen under the semaphore signals at Ely as Multiple Aspect Signalling (MAS) and track rationalisation were soon to be introduced under the electrification programme.

Top: **The first working of the weekend was the *'Golden Arrow'* from Cambridge to Kings Lynn. I suggest that this was the first and only time the *'Arrow'* was ever formed of a support coach and a three car Metro Cammell DMU set. The Metro Cammell set worked back as a scheduled train.**

Middle: *Taw Valley* **stands at Downham Market following a run past and photographic stop. The number of people who had come to see the trains, coupled with the short platforms at the wayside stations and the difficulties of detraining passengers, curtailed any further 'run pasts'. Sunday 20th October 1991.**

Bottom: **Taw Valley was shunted into Kings Lynn Sidings in order to run around its support coach and await *Britannia* with the first train proper. Here *Taw Valley* passes Kings Lynn Junction signal box on Saturday 19th October 1991.**

ASHFORD TO HASTINGS

As part of the 'Ashford 150' celebrations, a series of steam shuttles along the predominantly single line route from Ashford to Hastings was arranged. The locomotives were BR Standard Class 4 75069 (from the SVR) and *Taw Valley*. *Taw Valley* was to be used on the Saturday specials with 75069 being in action on the Sunday. When not in use, the locomotives were on display with No. 777 *Sir Lamiel* at the open days at Ashford Chart Leacon. As a finale to the weekend, a 'special' was arranged from Ashford to London Bridge with 'unusual motive power'. The special was to be run after dark. This was the start of a series of firsts for *Taw Valley* on the 'third rail' network.

Top right: **Chart Leacon in BR steam days ? No – Chart Leacon on Saturday 6th June 1992!** *Taw Valley* **stands with preserved Hastings power car S60001 from Unit 1001 and alongside, the 4-SUB No.4732. The weather during both days was overcast and wet (typical of the English summer). The sun eventually broke through late on the Sunday afternoon.**

Centre right: **The emergence of ex-BR Class 71 E5001, from the NRM, for restoration, was an added bonus at the open day. Here** *Taw Valley* **stands alongside the Class 71 at the entrance to the works on Saturday 6th June 1992. Note the derailers on the rails in front of the locomotives, protecting the entrance.**

Bottom: **34028** *Eddystone*!!! **The locomotive was renamed and renumbered on one side only, as a favour to the Eddystone Group. The group had assisted the** *Taw Valley* **support crew on various occasions whilst the locomotive was resident in the south east. Sunday 7th June 1992.** Antony Guppy.

Left: **Both locomotives worked tender first from Ashford and were hence smokebox first out of Hastings up the 1 in 60 climb to Ore Tunnel. Here,** *Taw Valley* **runs around the stock at Hastings, past some superb SR semaphore signals, on Saturday 6th June 1992.**

Below: **SR semaphore signals are rapidly becoming rarities. Thankfully, some were still to be seen around Hastings as** *Taw Valley* **waits 'for the off' at the head of the first return service to Ashford. A 4-CEP unit can be seen to the right on a service from Eastbourne.**

Bottom: **Taw Valley works tender first with a Hastings bound train on Saturday 6th June 1992.** K.J.C.Jackson

Above: The 'unusual motive power' for the evening special to London Bridge was, of course, *Taw Valley*. Thus did the engine break the long-standing ban which had prevented steam locomotives from being used on Southern tracks electrified on the third rail system. The locomotive is seen resting near the buffer stops at London Bridge after bringing in the special. The train was greeted throughout the journey by astonished onlookers as she sped up the main line via Tonbridge and Sevenoaks, and by a barrage of flash-lights as she eased across the pointwork into the terminus on Sunday 7th June 1992.

Right: The crew stand in celebration on the frontplate of *Taw Valley*. Left to right: Driver Bob Fleet, Inspector Noddy Forbes and Fireman Dave Lea. Bob Fleet suffered a mild stroke soon after the run and has since retired. Our very best wishes go out to both Bob and his family for a complete recovery and a long and happy retirement.

Below: Shortly after *Taw Valley* arrived, a second steam-hauled service drew into the platform alongside. This train was hauled by 75069. Here, *Taw Valley* and the standard Class 4 stand side by side at London Bridge on this occasion. Antony Guppy.

FROM EASTLEIGH TO EXETER

Top: The three locomotives involved in the Ashford open days and the London Bridge trip, finally ran as a triple header via Hither Green to the works at Eastleigh. Here, *Taw Valley* and *Sir Lamiel* stand in the sunshine, outside the Works on 9th June 1992.

Centre: On Wednesday 10th June 1992, *Taw Valley* is examined before taking out the test train from Eastleigh to Exeter Central with 75069. The sanders can be seen in operation.

Left: The sight of a steam locomotive on the West of England line still brings out the populace. Here, the school children of Gillingham, line the platform as the locomotives wait in the passing loop for an 'up' service to clear the single track section ahead, on Wednesday 10th June 1992.

Right and centre: **The locomotives are shunted into the bay on the 'up' side of Exeter Central Station, for attention. I wonder what the inmates of Exeter Prison thought of the proceedings, on Wednesday 10th June 1992?**

Bottom left: **The locomotives were inspected inside the main workshop at Eastleigh. Here, *Taw Valley* stands alongside a modern Class 442 'Wessex' EMU, on Saturday 20th June 1992.**

Bottom right: **A series of shuttles were run from Eastleigh to Salisbury, concurrently with the trips to Exeter. This was the duty of the locomotive not being used on the West of England route that day. As well as the three locomotives in action, repatriated ex-LSWR/SR/BR Class M7 0-4-4T 30053 was to be on display at Salisbury. The locomotive had been passed for BR running, and proved so popular that a series of short brake van trips around the Laverstock Loop were put on. Here, 30053 and *Taw Valley* stand side by side at Eastleigh Works, on Saturday 20th June 1992.**

Left: **The superb condition of *Taw Valley* can be seen in this shot, with *Sir Lamiel*, in Eastleigh Works' Yard on Saturday 20th June 1992.**

Centre left: **The locomotives involved on the trips to Exeter had to go to Yeovil Junction to turn. Here, *Taw Valley* is turned on the turntable at Yeovil Junction on Sunday 21st June 1992.**

Centre right: **The inaugural working from Andover to Exeter was entrusted to *Taw Valley*. A 20 minute late start turned into an on-time arrival at Exeter. Here, *Taw Valley*, resplendent with the 'Atlantic Coast Express' headboard, moves slowly onto the support coaches in Central Station after the run on Sunday 21st June 1992.**

Bottom: **A Regional Railways Class 158 passes *Taw Valley* as the locomotive leaves Salisbury for Eastleigh on Sunday 28th June 1992.** Brian Morrison.

BOURNEMOUTH

The highlight of the 1992 steam preservation year was the first public run of a steam hauled service from a former Southern Railway London terminus. *Taw Valley*, together with 75069, had been invited to appear at the open day at Bournemouth TrainCare Depot during September 1992.

After the trip from Ashford to London Bridge, the 34027 Taw Valley Group was able to promote, on their own behalf, an after-sunset trip from London Waterloo to Bournemouth. This would be the last leg of moving the engine from its summer season on the SVR to Bournemouth. It also allowed the 25th Anniversary of the cessation of steam working from Waterloo to be celebrated, or at least commiserated, in style.

It was a tremendous thrill for the whole of the support crew and passengers, for on emerging from the tunnel into Bournemouth Station, they were greeted by an estimated 4,000 people on the platforms, even at 2300hrs. The sight of 'wall-to-wall' people, even across the footbridge, with all those flashguns being fired, is a sight that will always be remembered.

The locomotive, on leaving Bournemouth, travelled down to Poole in order to run around its support coach, before proceeding into the Bournemouth TrainCare Depot

Top: ***Taw Valley* was shedded at Wimbledon East Depot overnight on Thursday 10th September 1992. Here, the locomotive undergoes an examination in the depot. Such was the interest that a crew from Sky Television arrived to film the proceedings. They can be seen on the walkway in the middle of the picture, on Friday 11th September 1992.**

Centre: **No words are needed to describe this picture, taken from the flats over-looking the entrance to Waterloo on Friday 11th September 1992. Brian Morrison.**

Bottom: **Driver Rodney White and Fireman Len Shave look back from the cab of *Taw Valley* as a 4-VEP and a Class 455 EMU enter Waterloo. Many of the older locomen were moved to tears to see the sight of a Bulleid awaiting 'the right away' for Bournemouth, after so many years. Once again, the date is 11th September 1992.**

Above: **The locomotive was taken off the train and put on the buffer stops on platform 14, in order to top up the tender tank. Many home-bound commuters could not believe their eyes as *Taw Valley* stood, in steam, and eventually moved out under her own power onto the awaiting stock.**

Left: **Bert Hitchen and Steve McColl stand by *Taw Valley* in the late evening sunshine on Friday 11th September 1992.**

Below: **Once again, no description is needed for this shot, taken from the flats overlooking Waterloo – only a reiteration of the date: Friday 11th September 1992.** Antony Guppy.

Above left: **The train left Waterloo some thirteen minutes late. As the special was routed between consecutive 'Wessex Electric' services, SR Control had intimated that there should be no delay caused by the train. The crew needed no further encouragement and Basingstoke was reached sufficiently quickly for an on-time departure. Roger Cruse, Bert Hitchin and the Driver check the motion and top up the oil during the Basingstoke stop.**

Above right: **The arrival at Bournemouth on Friday 11th September 1992 was a minute or two down, though what a greeting awaited! As mentioned earlier,** approximately 4,000 people thronged onto the platform and overbridge. Photography was almost an impossibility as this shot of the locomotive, taken a minute or so after arrival, shows.

Right: **The only available place for a photograph was from the tender. Taken a mere five minutes after arrival, spectators throng around the locomotive as the Inspector, and crew member Roger Scanlon, gaze onto the gathered crowd.**

Below: **The locomotive is seen here on display at the TrainCare Depot at Bournemouth on Sunday 13th September 1992.**

RETURN TO WATERLOO

After the run out of Waterloo to Bournemouth on 11th September, Taw Valley was booked to haul the first public working of a steam train into Waterloo since 9th July 1967. The run was to have taken place in February 1993 but had to be postponed until Easter Saturday, 10th April 1993.

Below: *Taw Valley* ran overnight from Southall via Reading and Basingstoke and it was noted in the down bay at Salisbury by 0700hrs on 10th April. After using the turntable at Yeovil Junction she is seen here awaiting 'the off' on the return leg. For once, a headboard was not carried, only the Southern headcode for a West of England express.

Bottom: **On the down trip, passengers were offered the opportunity to visit and spend a few hours in the beautiful Dorset town of Sherborne instead of carrying on to Yeovil Junction. The locomotive is seen standing at Sherborne on the return leg, with some local admirers. Indeed, with sufficient support from both locals and Network SouthEast, there appears to be a good case for a steam service between Salisbury and Yeovil during the summer season.**

Opposite page, top and bottom: **On the return leg, a break of three hours was taken at Salisbury, waiting for darkness to fall and preparing the locomotive for the final leg to Basingstoke and Waterloo. Once the train had arrived in Basingstoke, a short stop was made to ensure a path was made available to the Capital. It soon was, and the special was whisked away from Basingstoke to a stop in platform 13 at Waterloo in a time of 48 minutes for the 48 miles, stop to stop. It was also the first steam special to be timed at 75 mph, made possible by the provision of an Automatic Warning System (AWS) on *Taw Valley*. Here, *Taw Valley* stands simmering at the buffer stops, some 36 minutes early.**

Chapter Seven

SHACKERSTONE

Taw Valley had no booked work over the summer of 1993 so an offer from the Birmingham Railway Museum to hire the locomotive for driver training courses based at Shackerstone was accepted. Known as the 'Battlefield Line' the Shackerstone Railway Society owns the 4.5 mile line in southwest Leicestershire. The line follows the course of the Ashby-de-la-Zouch canal and terminates in the villages of Shackerstone at the north and Shenton in the south with Market Bosworth mid-way. Although double track in BR days the line is now single throughout with run around facilities at the three stations. Shenton is the site of the last battle in the Wars of the Roses, the Battle of Bosworth.

Taw Valley made the journey to Shackerstone from Southall via Didcot and Tyseley over the weekend of April 24th/25th. After a couple of weeks on Tyseley whilst the support crew prepared her for the trip to Shackerstone, the locomotive was loaded onto the low loader during the week beginning Monday 3rd May and transportation was arranged for the following Friday.

Top: *Taw Valley* **rests with larger sister ex-SR Merchant Navy 35005** *Canadian Pacific* **at Tyseley. 35005 was also on driver training duties at Tyseley, having been brought over from the Great Central Railway at Loughborough. Sunday 25th April 1993.**

Centre: **The entrance onto the railway proper is via the old trackbed just to the north of the station at Shackerstone. Here** *Taw Valley* **edges under one of the old road bridges as she approaches journey's end. The clearance under this bridge was about 2 inches above the chimney. Once in position the tractor unit was removed and the volunteer workers on the railway began the task of putting in the temporary track panels in order to unload her.**

Bottom: **When the panels were in place the railway's resident Ruston & Hornsby 0-4-0 DE shunter and match wagon coupled up to the locomotive and pulled** *Taw Valley* **off the low loader and onto the track. Here the ensemble stands on** *terra firma* **at Shackerstone, Friday 7th May 1993.**

Above: **The tender was delivered later the same Friday and was coupled up by Tyseley staff during the following week. The first weekend of working was to be 15th 16th May 1993 and here *Taw Valley* is seen running around its train at Shackerstone on Saturday 15th May.**

Below: **The driver training train was composed of three coaches, a Mk.1 SO, a Mk.1 BSK and an old LMS full brake. Trainees were given tuition in guard, fireman and driver's duties during their time on the railway. Here it awaits 'the off' at Shackerstone on 15th May 1993.**

Appendices

VARIOUS TAW VALLEY TIMINGS
1954, 1991 &1992

ATLANTIC COAST EXPRESS, 1954

The following article appeared in *Railway Magazine* in the October 1954 issue. Our thanks go to the Editor for permission to reproduce it here.

'At this point . . . unusually fine Southern Region runs over the main line from Exeter to Waterloo . . . timed by Mr A.Lathey, the up 'Atlantic Coast Express' rather unusually was handled out of Exeter by a 'West Country' Pacific No. 34027 *Taw Valley*, and the run once again demonstrates the exceptional capability of a locomotive which for a long time was rated no higher than Power Class '6', but which has since been promoted to '7P5F'. The 11 coach load weighed 358 tons tare, 375 tons gross.

'To Sidmouth Junction, reached in 30 seconds under the 18 minute schedule, the run was without incident. Then the engine went up the long 1 in 100-90 past Honiton at a minimum of 31 mph on each stage, duly eased down the bank for Seaton Junction and touched 84 at the bottom of the dip before Axminster. But it was after an exceptionally severe permanent way slowing at Chard Junction that the engine made such a superlative show.

'Reaching 85 mph below Crewkerne, *Taw Valley* rushed the broken grades to milepost 126.5 (partly at 1 in 120 up) at a minimum of 70.5 mph, and was doing just over 80 through Sherborne - a very unusual speed here in this direction. This made it possible to breast the succeeding 2 miles at 1 in 80 at a minimum of 55.5 mph, and to get up to 91 below Templecombe, so that the 24.0 miles from Crewkerne to milepost 107.5 were run off in 19 min. 14 sec. Now came a second bad permanent way check, and at another unfortunate location, immediately before the steep climb from Gillingham to Semley. Nevertheless *Taw Valley* accelerated up the 1 in 130-114-100 to 46 mph with a slight falling off to 44.5 at the top, and then fairly streaked away for Salisbury, reaching 86 mph before the Wilton curve slowing. Thus the engine had kept dead time on this difficult 79 minute booking, and the next time was certainly not more than 73 minute for the 75.8 miles of these mountainous grades'.

Dist		Sched	Actual	Speeds
miles		min/sec	min/sec	mph
00.0	EXETER CENTRAL	–	00.00	–
01.1	Exmouth Jct	–	04.20	17.5
04.8	Broad Clyst	–	08.57	67.0
08.5	Whimple	–	12.36	53/43
12.2	SIDMOUTH JUNCTION	18.00	17.29	47.5 (1)
04.6	HONITON	–	07.56	31/35.5
06.0	Honiton Tunnel West End	–	10.26	31/77.5
11.6	Seaton Junction	–	15.46	68.0*
14.8	AXMINSTER	–	18.15	84.0
		–	p.w.s	69.5/13*
19.9	Chard Junction	–	23.17	54.5 (2)
26.1	Milepost 133.25	–	33.04	50.5
27.9	Crewekerne	–	34.49	85.0
34.5	Sutton Bingham	–	39.49	70.5
36.7	YEOVIL JUNCTION	38.00	41.35	79/77.5
41.3	Sherborne	–	45.07	80.5
45.0	Milborne Port	–	48.35	55.5
47.4	TEMPLECOMBE	48.00	50.45	91.0 (3)
51.9	Milepost 107.5	–	54.03	69/73
		–	p.w.s	20.0*
54.2	Gillingham	–	57.02	–
58.3	Semley	–	62.58	44.5
63.3	Tisbury	–	67.27	78.5/74
67.6	Dinton	–	70.45	80.5/86
73.3	Wilton	–	75.06	51.0*
75.8	SALISBURY	79.00	79.09	–

Notes:
* = Speed restriction (curve, permanent way caution or signals).
(1) – At milepost 158 after restart.
(2) – Maximum between Chard Jct. and MP 133.25.
(3) – At Abbey Ford

THE ROYAL SCOTSMAN, 1991

Date: 28th December 1991
Route: Bradford Forster Square to Carlisle.
Weather: Dull with persistent drizzle, wind gusty.
Load: 10 coaches, 352 tons tare, 375 tons gross.

Milepost	Time	Qtr	Avge Speed	Remarks
225.00	00.00	00.00	(mph)	Gargrave Station
.25	00.24	00.24	37.00	
.50	00.49	00.25	36.00	
.75	01.14	00.25	36.00	
226.00	01.39	00.25	36.00	
.25	02.03	00.24	37.00	
.50	02.27	00.24	37.00	
.75	02.51	00.24	37.00	
227.00	03.13	00.22	41.00	
.25	03.37	00.24	37.00	
.50	03.59	00.22	41.00	
.75	04.22	00.23	39.00	
228.00	04.44	00.22	41.00	Bell Busk
.25	05.06	00.22	41.00	
.50	05.29	00.23	39.00	
.75	05.51	00.22	41.00	
229.00	06.15	00.24	37.00	
.25	06.38	00.23	39.00	
.50	07.02	00.24	37.00	
.75	07.28	00.26	35.00	(Summit)
230.00	07.51	00.23	39.00	
.25	08.13	00.22	41.00	
.50	08.33	00.20	45.00	
.75	08.51	00.18	50.00	
231.00	09.09	00.18	50.00	
.25	09.24	00.15	60.00	Hellifield Station
.50	09.40	00.16	56.00	
.75				
232.00	10.10	00.30	(60.00)	
.25	10.25	00.15	60.00	
.50				
.75	10.54	00.29	(62.00)	
233.00	11.08	00.14	64.00	
.25	11.22	00.14	64.00	
.50	11.34	00.12		
.75	11.48	00.14	64.00	
234.00	12.01	00.13		
.25	12.13	00.12		
.50	12.25	00.12		
.75	12.38	00.13		Settle Junction
235.00				
.25				
.50				
.75	13.32	00.54		
236.00	13.48	00.16	56.00	
.25				
.50				Settle
.75	14.37	00.49	(54.50)	
237.00	14.54	00.17	53.00	
.25	15.12	00.18	50.00	
.50	15.32	00.20	45.00	(slipped)
.75	15.52	00.20	45.00	
238.00	16.13	00.21	43.00	
.25	16.37	00.24	37.00	(slipped)
.50	17.00	00.23	39.00	

Milepost	Time	Qtr	Avge Speed	Remarks
238.75	17.23	00.23	39.00	Taitlands Tunnel
239.00	17.50	00.27	33.00	(slipped)
.25	18.17	00.27	33.00	
.50	18.46	00.29	31.00	(slipped)
.75	19.13	00.27	33.00	
240.00	19.43	00.30	30.00	
.25	20.12	00.29	31.00	
.50	20.42	00.30	30.00	
.75	21.12	00.30	30.00	
241.00	21.42	00.30	30.00	Helwith Bridge
.25	22.08	00.26	35.00	
.50	22.33	00.25	36.00	
.75	22.59	00.26	35.00	
242.00	23.26	00.27	33.00	(slipped)
.25	23.53	00.27	33.00	
.50	24.20	00.27	33.00	Horton-in-Ribblesdale
.75	24.48	00.28	32.00	
243.00	25.15	00.27	33.00	
.25	25.45	00.30	30.00	(slipped)
.50	26.15	00.30	30.00	
.75	26.45	00.30	30.00	
244.00				
.25				
.50	28.17	01.32	(29.00)	(slipped)
.75	28.52	00.35	26.00	
245.00	29.27	00.35	26.00	Selside
.25	30.03	00.36	25.00	
.50	30.42	00.39	23.00	
.75	31.19	00.37	24.00	
246.00	32.01	00.42	21.50	(slipped)
.25	32.42	00.41	22.00	
.50	33.25	00.43	21.00	
.75	34.08	00.43	21.00	
247.00	34.52	00.44	20.50	
.25	35.37	00.45	20.00	Ribblehead Station
.50	36.12	00.35	26.00	
.75				
248.00	37.34	01.22	(21.00)	
.25				
.50	39.07	01.33	(19.50)	
.75	39.57	00.50	18.00	Blea Moor Box
249.00	40.48	00.51	18.00	
.25	41.41	00.53	17.00	

Section	Time (min/sec)	Avge Speed (mph)
234.75 - 249.25	29.05	29.91
225.00 - 229.75	7.28	38.00
229.75 - 234.75	5.10	58.00

The run was undertaken on a dull overcast day with fine drizzle, especially after Skipton and up to Blea Moor, with a chill gusty wind.

After the stop at Skipton for a crew change the locomotive was worked steadily, and climbed to the summit beyond Bell Busk at MP 239.75 on a rising grade of 1 in 165-150-300-132-197 at an average speed of some 38 mph with a maximum of 41 mph. The dash down the grades of 1 in 214-181 through Hellifield was however taken in some style. The weather soon took its toll on the locomotive with slipping occuring as soon as the quarry, shortly after passing Settle Station.

The passage of Taitland's Tunnel was taken extremely carefully and although slipping did occur, even with the sanders on, the driver kept the train moving at a good 30 mph. From Helwith Bridge the locomotive accelerated from a steady 30 mph to 36 mph until MP 242 where slipping reduced the speed to 32 mph. After the two short grades of 1 in 200, both near Horton-in-Ribblesdale, the locomotive suffered a constant fight against the rail conditions and slipping brought the train down to 20 mph by Ribblehead.

Boiler pressure was down to 140 lb.sq.in approaching the summit. The speed of the train was brought to a crawl past Blea Moor Box and was not improved upon until passing the summit in the tunnel. The rest of the run into Carlisle was undertaken without due concern with a right time arrival.

CUMBRIAN MOUNTAIN EXPRESS, 1992

It is an anomaly that for over 100 years of its life, the steam locomotive was something of an enigma. There have been many instances where a potentially sound and amply proportioned locomotive has not lived up to expectations. However by the application of 'modern' scientific principles and the utilisation of 'modern' equipment it became possible to plan and execute proper testing. These tests took place, initially, on service trains, where a given locomotive worked the same loads week in and week out, with the same crew and in as near constant conditions as possible – if indeed the British weather, grade of coal, standard of water and locomotive condition etc. could ever be constant! These carefully planned series of trials, with or without dynamometer cars, produced some interesting results. They were not always what were expected and in some cases wide variances were found.

During the later days steam locomotives were tested by progressively more and more scientific methods, whether on a test plant, e.g. Rugby, or by properly controlled road testing, e.g. Mr S.O.Ell at Swindon. It was not, therefore, until very late in the day that the performance characteristics of these machines were laid bare.

Fortunately for the preservation movement the railway authorities decided to publish the results in full. Comparisons can thus be made between the results then obtained and the results now being obtained and conclusions drawn. However absorbing the details of design and construction, or even redesign and reconstruction, may be, it is the end product – the work of the locomotive on the road; that is the ultimate criterion by which the design is judged.

Nowadays, the unofficial 'blue riband' is the ascent of the 'long drag' on the famous Settle & Carlisle line, most notably southbound. A set of figures for 34027 *Taw Valley* follows. They are not claimed to be accurate to the 'nth' degree nor do they give anywhere near as full a picture as those scientific tests did. They do, however, give a quantitive idea of the performance that may be expected, in this case from a rebuilt Bulleid Light Pacific, on a particular occasion over a given route.

Date: 8th February 1992.
Weather: Dull, overcast dry no wind.
Load: 10 coaches 350 tons tare 375 tons gross
Locomotive & Tender: 144 tons (including coal & water)
Crew: Driver: Alexander. Firemen: Kane & Finlinson
Inspector: McClelland

Location	Time	Qtr	Avge Speed	Remarks
277.25	00.00	00.00	(mph)	Appleby station
277.00	01.10	01.10	(26.00)	
276.75	01.43	00.33	27.00	
.50	02.10	00.27	33.00	
.25	02.32	00.22	41.00	
276.00	02.52	00.20	45.00	
275.75	03.08	00.16	56.00	
.50	03.23	00.15	60.00	
.25	03.39	00.16	56.00	Ormside Viaduct
275.00	03.53	00.14	64.00	
274.75	04.08	00.15	60.00	
.50	04.22	00.14	64.00	
.25	04.38	00.16	56.00	
274.00	04.53	00.15	60.00	
273.75	05.08	00.15	60.00	
.50	05.24	00.16	56.00	Helm Tunnel
.25				(loco eased)
273.00	05.56	00.32	(56.00)	
272.75	06.15	00.19	47.00	(locomotive slipped)
.50	06.33	00.18	50.00	
.25	06.51	00.18	50.00	
272.00	07.08	00.17	53.00	
271.75	07.28	00.20	45.00	
.50	07.45	00.17	53.00	
.25	08.04	00.19	47.00	Grisburn Viaduct
271.00	08.21	00.17	53.00	
270.75	08.39	00.18	50.00	
.50	08.57	00.18	50.00	
.25	09.14	00.17	53.00	
270.00	09.31	00.17	53.00	Crosby Garrett
269.75	09.48	00.17	53.00	
.50	10.04	00.16	56.00	Crosby Garrett Viaduct
.25	10.21	00.17	53.00	Crosby Garrett Tunnel
269.00				
268.75	10.51	00.30	(60.00)	
.50	11.06	00.15	60.00	Smardale Viaduct
.25	11.21	00.15	60.00	
268.00	11.37	00.16	56.00	
267.75	11.52	00.15	60.00	
.50	12.08	00.16	56.00	(loco eased for failed
.25	12.27	00.19	47.00	Kirkby Stephen dist. signal)

Location	Time	Qtr	Avge Speed	Remarks
267.00	12.56	00.29	31.00	
266.75	13.33	00.37	24.00	Kirky Stephen Station
.50	14.12	00.39	23.00	
.25	14.47	00.35	26.00	
266.00	15.16	00.29	31.00	
265.75	15.41	00.25	36.00	
.50	16.05	00.24	37.00	
.25	16.28	00.23	39.00	
265.00	16.52	00.24	37.00	
264.75	17.13	00.21	43.00	
.50				(loco slipped)
.25	17.57	00.44	(41.00)	Birkett Tunnel
264.00	18.20	00.23	39.00	
263.75	18.43	00.23	39.00	
.50	19.05	00.22	41.00	
.25	19.26	00.21	43.00	
263.00	19.44	00.18	50.00	
262.75	20.02	00.18	50.00	
.50	20.21	00.19	47.00	
.25	20.41	00.20	45.00	
262.00	21.01	00.20	45.00	
261.75	21.21	00.20	45.00	
.50	21.41	00.20	45.00	
.25	22.01	00.20	45.00	
261.00	22.21	00.20	45.00	Ais Gill Viaduct
260.75	22.41	00.20	45.00	
.50	23.01	00.20	45.00	
.25	23.22	00.21	43.00	
260.00	23.44	00.22	41.00	
259.75	24.04	00.20	45.00	Ais Gill Summit

Section	Time (min.sec)	Avg. Speed mph	Max. Speed mph
277.25 - 267.50	12.08	48.21	
277.25 - 259.75	24.04	43.63	
275.25 - 273.75	1.29	60.67	62.00
275.25 - 267.50	8.29	54.82	
275.25 - 260.00	20.05	45.56	62.00
275.25 - 259.75	20.25	45.55	
275.00 - 268.00	7.44 (7.50)	54.55 (53.61)	
275.00 - 267.00	9.03 (8.58)	53.04 (53.53)	

Note: 277.25 - Appleby Station   260.00 - Ais Gill
275.25 - South end of Ormside Viaduct (Start of 1:100 gradient)
Locomotive worked at 40-45% cutoff full regulator maximum. Maximum gradient taken as 1:100 (Gradient Profile). Boiler Pressure 240 - 250 lb per sq. in.
Figures in brackets are from 71000 20.7.91

THE BOURNEMOUTH LIMITED, 1992

Date: 11th September 1992
Load: 10 coaches, 364 tons tare, 390 tons gross.

Distance		Schedule	Actual (min/sec)	
00.0	Waterloo	00.00	00.00	
03.9	Clapham Junction	07.00	09.00	
07.3	Wimbledon		13.20	
12.0	Surbiton	16.30	17.50	
19.1	Weybridge		23.40	
21.7	West Byfleet		25.40	
24.4	Woking	28.30	27.50	
28.0	Brockwood		30.55	
31.0	MP31		33.30	estimated
33.2	Farnborough		35.25	
36.5	Fleet		38.00	
39.8	Winchfield		40.45	
42.2	Hook		42.50	
47.8	BASINGSTOKE	55.00	50.00	51 min net
00.0	BASINGSTOKE	00.00	00.00	
02.5	Worting Junction	05.00	05.35	
10.3	Micheldever		13.20	
18.8	Winchester	23.00	19.35	
21.9	Shawford		21.50	
		signal	stop	

Distance		Schedule	Actual	
			(min/sec)	
25.8	Eastleigh		31.30	
			sigs	
30.4	Northam Junction	37.00	40.45	
31.4	SOUTHAMPTON	42.00	44.05	35 min net
00.0	SOUTHAMPTON	00.00	00.00	
06.3	Lyndhurst Road		10.00	
13.6	Brockenhurst	16.00	16.35	
16.3	Sway		19.15	
19.3	New Milton		21.45	
21.8	Hinton Admiral		23.50	
25.3	Christchurch		26.50	
			sigs	
28.7	BOURNEMOUTH	36.00	33.30	33 min net

The following logs compare 34027 *Taw Valley* on a Waterloo-Bournemouth working with Merchant Navy (MN) logs taken from 1957 Waterloo-Bournemouth expresses stopping only at Southampton. An estimated time of passing Basingstoke, rather than the actual stop time, has been taken as 5 minutes after passing Hook. The time at the summit of MP 31 has also been estimated for *Taw Valley* as it was too dark to see the milepost itself.

It can be seen that *Taw Valley*'s times were very good up to MP 31. The 9.3 miles up an average gradient of about 1 in 330 from West Byfleet to the summit was taken in 7.50 minutes. The load is about a coach or so less than that allowed for the MNs, but given the extra capacity of the MNs it makes the comparison fair.

No proper comparison can be made on the run to Southampton because of *Taw Valley*'s signal stop at Eastleigh. However she did run very quickly down the grade of 1 in 252 from Litchfield tunnel through Micheldever to Shawford. The locomotive saved some 4 minutes on schedule from Worting Junction to Winchester.

On from Southampton the similarity between *Taw Valley*'s times and that of 35010 are almost identical as far as Christchurch. 35021, then in original condition, was slower but with a far heavier train. Overall it can be seen that the performance of *Taw Valley* in 1992 can stand comparison with the best the steam days could offer.

The *Taw Valley* log and the MN comparison courtesy of Mr D Proctor. The original MN logs courtesy of the Editor of *Railway Magazine*.

Dist.	Locomotive	34027	35020	35017	35018
	Date	1992	1957	1957	1957
	Load in tons	395	425	430	440
	Condition	Rebuilt	Rebuilt	Rebuilt	Rebuilt
			min/sec		
00.0	Waterloo	00.00	00.00	00.00	00.00
03.9	Clapham Junction	09.00	07.15	08.03	06.20
07.3	Wimbledon	13.20	11.18	12.11	10.13
12.0	Surbiton	17.50	16.07	17.01	14.40
19.1	Weybridge	23.40	22.28	23.21	20.48
21.7	West Byfleet	25.40			
24.4	Woking	27.50	27.05	28.21	25.18
28.0	Brookwood	30.55	30.29	32.05	28.45
31.0	MP 31	33.30+	33.23	35.11	31.48
33.2	Farnborough	35.25	35.25	37.21	33.57
36.5	Fleet	38.00	38.13	40.14	36.52
39.8	Winchfield	40.45	41.05	42.48	39.44
42.2	Hook	42.50	43.14	44.55	41.50
47.8	BASINGSTOKE	47.50*	48.17	49.20	46.42
	Average speeds	60.0	59.4	58.1	61.4

Dist.	Locomotive	34027	35017	35010	35021
	Date	1992	1957	1957	1957
	Load in tons	395	425	425	465
	Condition	Rebuilt	Rebuilt	Rebuilt	Orig
00.0	SOUTHAMPTON	00.00	00.00	00.00	00.00
06.3	Lyndhurst Road	10.00	10.00	9.49	10.30
13.6	Brockenhurst	16.35	16.45	16.44	18.07
16.3	Sway	19.15	19.26	19.02	21.42
19.3	New Milton	21.45	22.20	21.46	25.00
21.8	Hinton Admiral	23.50	24.33	23.47	27.34
25.3	Christchurch	26.50	27.18	26.33	30.45
		sigs	stop		
28.7	BOURNEMOUTH	33.30	35.58	32.09	35.40
	Net times	32.30	32.45	32.15	35.45
	Avge speeds, Lyndhurst Road to Christchurch	–	65.2	68.1	56.2

+ estimated time at MP 31.   * estimated time to pass Basingstoke